IS IT REALLY TRUE WHAT YOU HEAR IN THE PEW?

Ted Everett

ISBN 979-8-88832-567-4 (paperback)
ISBN 979-8-88832-568-1 (digital)

Christian Faith Publishing
832 Park Avenue
Meadville, PA 16335
www.christianfaithpublishing.com

Printed in the United States of America

ACKNOWLEDGMENTS

I would be remiss if I didn't mention my dearly departed parents for the example and discipline they provided. Although at the time it wasn't appreciated, they nurtured and helped me tremendously. Any credit that I may gain is only because of them. This world is a much better place because of them and the lives they had an impact on.

Turning thoughts into a book is very difficult. I want to thank my wife, Marsha, and my children for their help, patience, and opinions; it is a combined effort. Thanks be to God; I believe I have the best family!

Lastly, a very sincere thanks and extraordinary debt of gratitude to my niece, Dr. Audra Classen. Her support, encouragement, and editing were invaluable assets. You are a very special person and a real credit to our family, your generation, and this world.

INTRODUCTION

After being in the cemetery/funeral industry for close to thirty years, I begin to ask myself this question. See, I probably have heard more funeral sermons than most, and one day it dawned on me that in almost every funeral, the pastor assures the family that their loved one will live in heaven for eternity. This is comforting to the families, but according to scripture I had read, this is not true. Yes, I understand that in times of loss, some will say it is a pastor's job to comfort the family, but surely there were some who knew this may not be the case. The Bible teaches that some will spend eternity in hell, and common sense tells me not everyone is going to make it into heaven. Thus, I began to study and dig for myself, knowing that I am responsible for what I believe, and I will be the only one that will answer for my actions and beliefs at judgment. After many years of research and my own due diligence, the birth of this booklet was born.

The purpose of this book is to explain my understanding of what living a Christian life is supposed to be from my perspective. This perspective evolved from being raised in a Christian home with Christian parents. Parents that gathered around at the end of the day before bedtime, had a time of Bible reading and prayer. Each person prayed and told God what they wanted to tell Him, from the youngest to the oldest, with my dad closing it out after Mother prayed. In my family, spiritual matters required your respect for others and attention. Listening enabled you to help your loved ones pray for their concerns. With six children in the family, you had to be focused. If you fell asleep before it was your turn, you were reprimanded strongly.

My perspective not only comes from my early training but also from years of reading the Bible with the knowledge and belief that it is the inerrant, infallible, inspired Word of God. I firmly believe that if the Bible is properly studied and rightly divided, it will fit together similar to a jigsaw puzzle. That is two steps that should not be glossed over, studied, and rightly divided. There are several methods that can be used in studying scripture. One that I like is the SOAP method. If there is some scripture that you don't understand or you just may not be clear on, this may help. *S* is for "scripture"; write it down. *O* is for "observation"; observe things which the scripture may represent. *A* is for "application," how you can apply these observations to your life. *P* is for "prayer"—this is the most important. Ask God to show you the true meaning or an example in real life. Rightly dividing scripture is equally important. Another way of thinking about this is the old adage, "A text without a context is a pretext for a proof text." I would not advise anyone to take a single verse from scripture and make a doctrinal stand on that verse, especially if that verse is taken out of context. It is the big picture and how it all fits together. Use scripture to interpret and understand scripture. I believe if these steps are taken, when there seems to be contradictory scripture, this method can clarify ambiguities, align with other scripture, and make perfect sense.

Do not get me wrong, I do not have all of the answers; I am just a simple man without a whole lot of formal education. I went to school for thirteen years. No, I didn't fail a grade (LOL). I finished one year of college. Although that has been some years ago, I have endeavored to continue to learn new things and broaden my horizons, so to speak. Also, I am in no way trying to indicate that my knowledge of scripture is superior or that I can equate my understanding above anyone else, much less explain in my human frailty the mind of God. I do find it to be an interesting fact that Jesus, when He walked this earth, taught a simple gospel in a simple way. He cosigned the future of his church to a group of mostly unlettered men!

I am convinced that a lot of confusion exists based on what is preached and taught in most major denominations, compared to my understanding of what I read in the Holy Scriptures. Hopefully after reading this book with an open mind, studying scripture, and considering the content prayerfully, you will have a better understanding as to why I believe what I believe. You don't want to be like the older gentleman who said he knew a man once that was so narrow-minded that he could look through a keyhole with both eyes open (LOL)!

Let's take a little journey to our destination we will call "the House of Truth." As with any trip, there are several roads and maybe a detour or two that we may have to take before we finally get there.

ACCEPTED STREET

Before we get moving too fast down this street, I think it is a good idea to prepare for this journey of finding truth. My dad, a very wise man, used to say often, "To prevent a misunderstanding, you need to get a good understanding." There are some things a lot of people have to just agree to disagree upon and leave it there, but there are some things where, at some point, a line in the sand is drawn and you cannot be moved or there is no compromising. In an effort to mitigate some of that, I would like to lay out a few things that I think a majority of Christians can agree upon. Of course, this is not meant to be an exhaustive list by any means. This is just a starting point for which we can agree and we can move forward. If you do not agree on some of these more basic points, you may not find this book to be as helpful as I have intended and may want to read some fictional or romantic novel.

First, most people that I refer to as Christian will accept the following facts. As recorded in scripture, (a) Jesus was born of a virgin, (b) lived a sinless life on earth, (c) after his death on the cross, rose from the grave and triumphed over death, hell, and the grave. If we can agree on these three facts, then we have found a starting point. This means, to some degree, we are on the same road/ journey. If we cannot agree on these facts at this juncture, then it may be impossible for you to appreciate the rest of the journey. However, by starting with some general area of agreement, you can endeavor to see exactly where the divergent may happen and study to see if, after further consideration and examination, your precepts may have been influenced more based on what Bro. So-and-So said, rather than actual scripture text. It has been stated that it is easier to find a church/pastor to fit into what we believe, rather than studying scripture and praying for understanding and finding a church/pastor that preaches the gospel according to the scripture.

We are commanded by God in 2 Timothy 2:15 to "Study to show thyself approved unto God a workman that needeth not to be ashamed rightly dividing the word of truth." Also, 1 John 4:1 tells us, and he is talking to Christians, "Beloved, believe not every spirit, but try the spirits whether they are of God: because many false prophets are gone out into the world." These are only a couple of the many scriptures that I am basing my cautions on regarding false prophets/pastors. Another is in Matthew 24:4, "And Jesus answered them, 'See that no one leads you astray,'" There are several more scriptures with similar warnings (e.g., Romans 16:18) that sound an alarm, but for the sake of space and time, you get the point. We will all be held accountable for what saith the Word of God, not what Bro. So-and-So said. We are to make sure that we know, we know—not "I think so"! As we move further along our journey, we have to get on the main highway.

COMMON HIGHWAY

I feel most Christians will agree that we need to repent of our sin because scripture tells us in Romans 3:23, "For all have sinned and come short of the glory of God." This problem called *sin* has to be dealt with if we plan on going to heaven. All humans have problems too numerous to list, but the root cause of most all of our problems can be traced to this thing called *sin*. Its first cause was human disobedience, and its end is death. As stated in Romans 6:23, "For the wages of *sin* is death, but the free gift of God is eternal life in Christ Jesus our Lord." *Sin* is basically a biblical term and has to do with man and his relationship with God. Pretty much everything else concerning human difficulties has its roots in *sin*.

Now, concerning sin, let me go down a little detour. A lot of people today want to blame God when bad things happen. It goes something like this, "If there is a God, why do bad things happen to good people?" If there is a fire, flood, or other such disaster, people want to blame God. Scripture tells us that good things come from God. In James 1:17, "Every good gift and every perfect gift is from above, coming down from the Father of lights with whom there is no variation or shadow due to change." See, maybe just because they don't know scripture, they blame God. Now when the opposite happens and things are going great, some call it "lucky" or "fortunate"; most don't call it "blessed." Again, I like to keep things simple. The devil's job or main objective is to kill, steal, and destroy (e.g., John 10:10). If something is bad, blame the devil, not God. When it is good, give God the credit! Enough of that; let's get back on the highway.

When dealing with *sin*, sometimes I think most people will paint with a broad brush. In the matter of *sin*, I find it interesting. The Bible never regards the human race as merely unfortunate, although there are indications all through the Bible of divine pity (e.g., Job 6:14, Joel 2:18, etc.). The Bible always treats man as guilty and therefore destined to punishment. The fact of sin's presence is attributed to the fact of a fall and the effect of that fall extending to the entire race. See, the fall of man, as described in Genesis 3, is not the result of any flaw in God's creation; the flaw is in our response to His commands. According to God's plan, man was the crowning achievement of His creative activity. Matter-of-fact, God looked upon it and saw that it was "very good" (e.g., Genesis 1:31). Not long after that, paradise was soon marred by the intrusion of sin, which severed the peaceful and happy relationship between God and man. This event is referred to as "the fall of man." By disobeying God's word, man brought upon himself the curse of God and was driven out of Eden. Genesis 6 tells us, "And it repented the Lord that He had made man on the earth, and it grieved Him at His heart." If we keep reading, we see where God decided to destroy everything, including man, from the face of the earth. This tells us a lot about what God thinks of sin. It is serious business!

Before we get into talking about *sin* too much, it would be good to know a definition of *sin*. This seems like a simple thing, and it is a very important thing because this is what separates us from God. Interestingly, I have asked a number of people a simple question, can you give me a one-sentence definition of *sin*? Most are what I call church-goers, some were preacher's kids, and some were preachers' wives. Even though it doesn't sound that difficult, some seem to have a hard time giving a good definition. Some wanted to start naming certain sins (i.e., murder, rape, etc.) and I had to reiterate—not what *is* sin but a *definition of* sin. It is important what people believe because, for most people, belief determines behavior. I believe a good biblical definition is given in James 4:17: "Therefore to him that knoweth to do good, and doeth it not, to him it is sin."

For years, a number of theological names have been used for this inward sin principal, such as original sin, inbred sin, and indwelling sin. These are not the exact phraseologies of scripture, yet they come close to what most believe what scripture is teaching. This is what some refer to as the sinful nature. If you follow this line of thinking, then I think it is safe to believe that we are born with this sinful nature. Also, over and above this, I believe, based on scripture, that man is sinful in another way. We commit sinful acts. Therefore, we are sinful in two ways: (1) Sinful nature and (2) sinful acts. I understand that the sinful acts are the outcome of the sinful nature, yet the sinful acts are done by our own choice. This can be referred to as actual sin or the acts of sin committed. Hence, in general scripture usage, sinful acts are set forth in plural nouns such as *sins, iniquities*, etc. This is in contrast with the singular nouns *sin* and *iniquity*, which refer more to the sinful nature/inherited sin. Sinful acts can also be termed "the works of the flesh" as in Galatians 5:19–21.

Here then is our problem—*sin*, inherited and committed. I think most Christians understand about Adam's fall and our inherited sin, so let's look a little closer at sins committed. How does that happen or what is the progression? This is addressed in James 1:14–15, where scripture tells us, "But each person is tempted when he is lured and enticed by his own desires. Then desire when it has conceived gives birth to sin, and sin when it is fully grown brings forth death." As we see, *sin* starts from our inherited roots and then progresses. Let's drill down a little further in this vein.

A. Progression of Sin

First, notice in verse 14 toward the end that it starts with *desire*. This is that inherited part of sin. We all have the desire for/to sin in our spiritual DNA. Each person's desire may be different, but the devil knows my weakness and yours. Therefore, we need to know what our weakness is and own it, take responsibility for it, and not try and blame others for it! Notice scripture says "his own lusts." It is your own desires that cause you to sin. If you didn't desire it, you wouldn't do it. Our compulsion to sin comes from inside each of us. Jesus said so in Matthew 15:19–20, "For out of the heart come evil thoughts, murder, adultery, sexual immorality, theft, false witness, slander. These are what defile a person." This is in agreement with the above scripture we quoted in James. It is not the devil's fault, it is not someone else's fault, and scripture tells us it certainly isn't God's fault. The narrative today is to blame others or make excuses. Some will say things like, "My parents abused me," or "I was bullied at school when I was younger," etc. Today everyone needs to *own it, not excuse it!* The desire comes from our own heart. We are tempted when we have a desire for it; scripture says, "lured and enticed." Satan knows what you have fallen for before, and he chooses the bait that you find attractive.

The second stage in this process is *deception*. Part of deception is that *sin* always looks or sounds good in the beginning or on the outside. Another part of the deception is the lies we tell ourselves (i.e., "No one will know," "Just this once," "I deserve a little fun every now and then," "Everyone sows a few wild oats," "I can stop anytime," or one of my favorites I have heard before, "I'll ask forgiveness tomorrow," and many such others). This is why Jesus tells us in verse 16, "Do not be deceived, my beloved brothers." Deception is always a part of the process. We know sin is not right, and we should not be doing whatever *sin* it is. We know the guilt and emptiness we may feel later, but we lie and deceive ourselves again. Also, most of us have heard pastors from the pulpit tell us that no one is perfect—we all sin some every day. Is this true based on scripture, or is this part of the devil's deception?

The third stage is *disobedience*. What begins in our mind and is dwelled upon moves into actions and behavior. Our scripture verse in James 1:15 told us, "Then desire when it has conceived gives birth to sin." Of course, an example of this is when King David spied a woman bathing. He desired her, but if at that point he would have turned away and perhaps knelt down in prayer to God, it may have been over in a matter of moments. We know he didn't do that. He decided to carry it just a little further. Maybe he told himself, "I'll just inquire and see who she is." He was told not only that she was married, but he knew who she was married to, one of his best soldiers. He desired her, he invited her to his chamber, and we know the rest of the story. The evil fantasy that was conceived in his heart gave birth (literally) to sin in his behavior. He decided to disobey after maybe listening to himself that, because he was king, he could get away with it, or no one would ever know. He willfully knew it was wrong and did it anyway. This was a sinful act/committed sin.

The fourth and final stage is *death*. It was death for Adam and Eve. It was death for David. It is death for us. We need to understand that Adam, Eve, and David didn't die immediately but their relationship with God did. It is always death; every time we die just a little bit more. The stakes are extremely high, even to our health, conscience, and well-being. Let's look at the verse just above our passage verse, James 1:12, "Blessed is the man that endureth temptation: for when he is tried, he shall receive the crown of life, which the Lord hath promised to them that love him." James is telling us that if we endure and persevere, we will receive the crown of life. He is also telling us, indirectly, that if we fail or give in to the flesh (sin), we receive death. See the choice is always our choice. We choose life (Christian living) or death (sinful living). We can't have it both ways.

B. Escaping Sin

Some people say escaping *sin* can't be done, and it can't without Jesus and the help of the Holy Spirit. Paul tells us in 1 Corinthians 10:13, "There hath no temptation taken you but such as is common to man: but God is faithful, who will not suffer you to be tempted above that ye are able; but will with the temptation also make a way to escape, that ye may be able to bear it." God and scripture do not lie, it is always our fault! As I have shown, we have time to think about what we do and scripture tells us He will make a way out, an escape. Keep in mind, we can't do it on our own; it is only with God's help. We are no match for the devil; that is why scripture tells us in Philippians 4:13, "I can do all things through Christ who strengthenth me." I have said it many times: scripture is like a jigsaw puzzle. If it is rightly divided and understood properly, it will not contradict itself, and everything will support and fit together as it should.

Another scripture text that a lot of people use to support their position of not being able to live without sinning, some every day, is in Romans chapter 7, where Paul says in verse 19, "For the good that I would I do not: but the evil which I would not, that I do." This is just one example of a verse in this chapter, but there are others also in this chapter that are used. If you look at some of these verses singularly, you can see how someone may misinterpret the point Paul is trying to make. However, if you take the whole chapter and read and understand within the context in which it is written, you will see that Paul is teaching them the difference—that people are no longer under the law but under grace. The law could not save them and keep them from sinning. We are no match for the devil; we are hopeless on our own. As was stated earlier in Philippians 4:13, "I can do all things through Christ which strengtheneth me." This is the only way we can live a life of Christian perfection—with Christ living within us. It is essential that we have the help, support, and guidance of the Holy Spirit. Also, if you keep reading in Romans chapter 8, Paul goes on further to try and sum up what he is teaching them. This is why it is imperative that we study and not just listen and believe everything that a preacher has been taught in seminary. You and you alone will have to give an account for your life, how you lived, and what you believed.

C. Modern versus Biblical View of Sin

We need to keep in mind that the biblical doctrine of *sin* is that it is a personal rebellion against God and an attempt on the part of the creature to be God in his own eyes. The modern attitude that *sin* is mere negation or absence of good, love, or opportunity is accordingly hostile to the biblical point of view. The modern view blames society, heredity, environments, parents, teachers, and anything but the will of man. The biblical point of view sees man as responsible for *sin*. It is not to be blamed on anyone or anything else. *Sin* is rebellion against God and the attempt to be one's own god—an attempt initiated by Satan and now continued in alliance with men. Satan cannot be blamed for *sin* though, man is responsible for his own guilt. *Sin* comes from a partnership, an alliance with Satan, not a helpless role. Therefore, love is not a cure-all for sin; a changed heart is required. Man's love is not the answer. It is only God in Jesus Christ and his cross, which is redemptive, which changes men into new creatures. We have to take the next exit.

PECULIAR ROAD

Now that we have an understanding of what *sin* is, how do we deal with it? As stated previously in Romans 3:23, "All have sinned." Many scriptures teach that we should repent. One example is in Acts 2:38, when Peter said, "Repent and be baptized every one of you in the name of Jesus Christ for the forgiveness of your sins, and you will receive the gift of the Holy Spirit." Again, I think scripture is pretty clear, and most Christians can agree repentance is necessary for the forgiveness of sins. Most refer to this as being "saved." A lot of fake Christians want God to save them (from pain, hell, and suffering), but God wants to be the Lord of their lives. He wants them to look to him for everything. There is a difference between the two.

Some may ask, what is repentance? Repentance is a personal, absolute, and ultimate unconditional surrender to God as sovereign. Though it includes sorrow and regret, it is more than that. In repenting, one makes a complete change of direction. A 180-degree turn toward God. Acts 3:19 says, "Repent therefore, and turn back, that your sins may be blotted out." Also, Acts 26:20b says, "Repent and turn to God."

A. Repentance at Work

Repentance is not something we can do on our own or just on a whim, so to speak. What I mean by this is, you have heard people say something like, "I am going to make a new year's resolution to do better," or "I am going to reform my life," or maybe they say something like, "I'm going to turn over a new leaf." There is nothing wrong with this kind of thinking, but this kind of thinking is about "I." Repentance comes when there is godly sorrow because of His convicting spirit. Repentance comes not on our time but on God's time when He knocks on your heart's door. Some people will say, "Well, 1 John 1:9 says, 'If we confess our sins, He is faithful and just to forgive us our sins, and to cleanse us from all unrighteousness.'" God's spirit brings us to the point of having a contrite spirit and broken heart. You may say, "Is this backed up by scripture?" Yes, it is. I believe we see exactly what I am talking about mentioned in Hebrews 12:16–17, "Lest there be any fornicator, or profane person, as Esau, who for one morsel of meat sold his birthright. For ye know how that afterward, when he would have inherited the blessing, he was rejected: for he found no place of repentance, though he sought it carefully with tears." Here we see where scripture tells us that Esau "sought it carefully with tears" and it also tells us "he found no place of repentance."

Also, look at John 6:44, "No man can come to me, except the Father which hath sent me draw him: and I will raise him up at the last day." There are more scriptures that support this but, for the sake of time and space, these should suffice. Lastly, God wants all to be saved, but scripture tells us His spirit will not always strive with us (e.g., Genesis 6:3).

B. Repentance In Action

Repentance is change! As a matter of fact, repentance literally means a change of mind. It involves the acknowledgment of guilt, of a deliberately false and wayward purpose, and a humble reversal of direction to follow the word of God. Repentance is therefore not merely regret for consequences but recognition of a perverse direction of the heart and a direction change in the heart. Change is not only required on the inside, in how we think or believe. Change should also be apparent in our outside actions (e.g., the way we live, act, talk, and behave). The Second Epistle to the Corinthians 5:17 says, "Therefore if any man be in Christ, he is a new creature: old things are passed away; behold all things are become new." Here is a problem: if someone says they have asked God for forgiveness and tells you they are saved, but they say that they still sin every day, where is the change? Sinning before you were saved and continuing to sin after you are saved makes no sense to me. This lifestyle is not supported by scripture. Remember, scripture will not contradict itself if properly understood and rightly divided. To justify their position on this matter, some people will say, "Well, they never got it in the first place," and this may be true. However, that person thought that they got the real thing and believed they did so based on what they heard from the pulpit. My simple understanding makes more sense and scripture will fit together like a jigsaw puzzle. We are all sinners, yet at some time, we are given a choice. If we choose to become a Christian and live the Christian lifestyle with Christ's help, we can live a life without sinning every day. In a nutshell, true repentance or conversion is regeneration, or rebirth and without repentance, man remains spiritually dead.

C. Repentance versus Sorrow

Another area that I think some people are a little confused about is the difference between true repentance and being sorrowful. A good example of this is in the scripture, and it occurred around the same time to two of Jesus's disciples. Read and study about Peter and Judas Iscariot (Peter from Luke chapter 22 and Judas from Matthew chapter 27). Both did wrong, but one repented and one was sorrowful—*big difference*! Repentance is necessary to receive God's forgiveness. *Grief without repentance can lead only to despair!* As we get closer to our destination, the road is starting to get narrow.

ROAD LESS TRAVELED

Most Christians can agree that once you have sincerely repented and asked Christ into your heart, you are a Christian. To be a Christian is to be Christlike. This is scriptural. The First Epistle of John 2:6 says, "He that saith he abideth in him ought himself also to walk, even as he walked." Who is He? He is Jesus! This sounds pretty straightforward and not too hard to understand, so how did Jesus walk/live? We know based on scripture that Jesus was a man without sin—*perfect*! So if I understand this, our goal and objective as Christians is to strive to live a life like Jesus did.

Can we live without sin? Most say no, and a few say yes, but in reality, it doesn't matter what *most* or *some* say—that is not how we are going to be judged. What we are going to be judged by is what the word of God says!

So let's look at some scriptures like 1 John 3:5. "And ye know that he was manifested to take away our sins; and in him is no sin." Let me say it again, this is our example, and this is the standard we are to strive to live by. Some may say this is just a rare verse maybe taken out of context, I say not so fast. Look at 1 John 3:6–9, "Whosoever abideth in him sinneth not: whosoever sinneth hath not seen him, neither known him. Little children, let no man deceive you: he that doeth righteousness is righteous, even as he is righteous.

He that committeth sin is of the devil; for the devil sinneth from the beginning. For this purpose the Son of God was manifested, that he might destroy the works of the devil. Whosoever is born of God doth not commit sin, for his seed remaineth in him: and he cannot sin, because he is born of God." *Wow*, I am not that smart, and I understand that. Similarly, 1 Corinthians 15:34 states, "Awake to righteousness, and sin not." All through these scriptures, you see righteousness associated with no sin.

What I am saying, and what I believe the Bible teaches, is that we are to live a life of Christian perfection, a life where we strive to live without sinning. This is what really gets a lot of people upset because they may not understand what I mean by this statement. Let me try and explain it to you. Yes we do and will continue to make mistakes as we are tempted, just as Jesus was tempted. Of course, all of this is backed by scripture. Let's again read James 1:14–15, "But every man is tempted, when he is drawn away of his own lust, and enticed. Then when lust hath conceived, it bringeth forth sin: and sin, when it is finished, bringeth forth death." These verses are talking about the relationship between temptation and sin. As I stated earlier, everyone will be tempted, but how we handle that temptation determines whether it is a sin or not. Also, while we are here in James, let's look at the admonition he gives us in the very next verse in James 1:16. "Do not err, my beloved brethren." Most scholars believe that in scripture where the term *brethren* is used, it is referring to Christians of that day. So remember that James is talking about temptation turning into sin, sin bringing forth death, and as an additional warning he adds, "*Do not err!*" Again, I hate to keep repeating myself, but he didn't leave room for error. He didn't say to not err too much, or that it is okay to err some; He simply said to not err. Even a simple man with not much understanding, like me, should be able to get that meaning.

Also, as an additional reference, I would like to look at Ezekiel 18:21–24, "But if the wicked will turn from all his sins that he hath committed, and keep all my statutes, and do that which is lawful and right, he shall surely live, he shall not die. All his transgressions that he hath committed, they shall not be mentioned unto him: in his righteousness that he hath done he shall live. Have I any pleasure at all that the wicked should die? Saith the Lord God: and not that he should return from his ways, and live? But when the righteous turneth away from his righteousness, and commitheth iniquity, and doeth according to all the admonitions that the wicked man doeth, shall he live? All his righteousness that he hath done shall not be mentioned: in his trespass that he hath trespassed, and in his sin that he hath sinned, in them shall he die."

Most Christians understand and accept the first part, believe that we are all sinners, and when we are saved, all our sins are thrown into the sea of forgetfulness to be remembered no more. That is exactly what the first part of that scripture says. What I find interesting is that they believe that God can forgive them for all the bad things they have done in their life, not even remember them. Their sins are gone and forgotten, and God wiped their slate clean, so to speak. However, they stumble at the thought of believing just the opposite. That no matter how much good you have done as a Christian, when you sin, God treats you the same as he did before you were saved. As the above scripture says, "All his righteousness that he hath done shall not be mentioned: in his trespass that he hath trespassed, and in his sin that he hath sinned, in them shall he die." Why is it so easy to believe the one and not the other? Folks, just because you may have never heard this before does not matter. I did not write the scriptures, I just read them!

A. Christian Perfection

We can live a life of Christian perfection because the Bible tells us about people that did. See Job 1:8, "And the Lord said unto Satan, 'Hast thou considered my servant Job, that there is none like him in the earth, a perfect and an upright man, one that feareth God, and escheweth evil?'" Here is where a lot of scholars will say the meaning of this word here means "mature" again. I am just a common man and understand it to mean what it says. Christian perfection/purity is different from Christian maturity. Maturity is not a condition for admittance into heaven, while purity is. The heart may be cleansed from all sin while the Christian is still immature. Purity has respect to moral cleanness or freedom from the defilement of sin. Maturity is a question of time and is subject to the laws of growth and development—as in the saying "Grow in grace." No Christian is cleansed into maturity, and none grow into purity. The Bible nowhere promises maturity as a work of God by faith, but purity, it does. Purity is received, maturity is acquired. Purity is received by faith, maturity is reached through time. Purity has to do with quality, maturity has to do with quantity.

We also see in the New Testament in Luke 1:6, where the scripture is talking about the mother and father of John the Baptist, and it says, "And they were both righteous before God, walking in all the commandments and ordinances of the Lord blameless." These are just a couple of examples in scriptures, but of course there are others.

Can we live this life today? I believe we can or God wouldn't have commanded us to. I do not think God would tell us to do something that we could not do, or He would be an unjust God! Let's read Matthew 5:48 where Jesus is finishing up with the Sermon on the Mount. He is getting close to the end, and listen to what He says, "Be ye therefore perfect, even as your Father which is in heaven is perfect." Should we have substituted "mature" here, as some might suggest? If so, the scripture would be saying that God in heaven was mature. I don't think that is the point that was being made here. I think "perfect" is a better description. Also, in John when the woman is caught in adultery and brought before Jesus to be stoned, you all know the story. Jesus told them, "He that is without sin among you, let him first cast a stone at her."

Of course, they all left, and in verse 11, Jesus tells her, "Neither do I condemn thee: go and sin no more." Surely he wouldn't tell her to do something she could not do, *no way*! There are other supporting scriptures that tell us to live a perfect life (e.g., 2 Corinthians 13:11, Colossians 1:28, 2 Timothy 3:17, Hebrew 6:1, and James 1:4) just to name a few.

Some say it can't be done, and it can't without Jesus and the help of the Holy Spirit. It is always our choice, and I don't make that statement lightly. I say that based on scripture found in 1 Corinthians 10:13 where it states, "There hath no temptation taken you but such as is common to man: but God is faithful, who will not suffer you to be tempted above that ye are able; but will with the temptation also make a way to escape, that ye may be able to bear it." See, if we are tempted to the point to where we have to sin some every day, then this verse is not true, and that cannot be the case. I believe the reason God designed it to be that way is because if we were tempted to the point where we were unable to bear it, then when we died and stood at judgment, we could blame God for the reason we sinned. God makes an escape so we can't blame him! Keep in mind, if we rightly divide the word of God, it will always fit together like a puzzle. An excellent measuring stick is that the Holy Scriptures will never contradict themselves. Often if there is a contradiction, the scriptures are not rightly divided, and we need to go to God in prayer and ask for a better understanding.

At this point, it needs to be stated that we are not talking about the same perfection as God. He stands alone and we cannot even come close to comparing ourselves to Him. He is omnipotent, omniscient, omnipresent, immutable, and eternal. These perfections are absolute, independent, and unrivaled. This implies freedom from all fault, mistakes, and errors. No sane person claims this type of perfection. Let me explain. In workmanship, a thing is regarded as perfect if it answers the purpose for which it was designed, whether it is a watch or a fountain pen. Watches do not write letters, and fountain pens do not give us the time of day. There is a limit for each, but within that limit, the purpose is realized and that is indicative of its perfection. If perfection is acknowledged within a wide range of things such as the above, why not the perfection of a Christian?

Remember, when we first started this discussion, how we said some people say sin is the transgression of the law. Well, if you remember the law, almost all of the commandments start out with "Thou shalt not..." Not much room for error there. He didn't say sometimes or a little but none!

B. Living Sacrifice

Let's look at what we are supposed to be according to Romans 12:1–2, "I beseech you therefore, brethren, by the mercies of God, that ye present your bodies a living sacrifice, holy, acceptable unto God, which is your reasonable service. And be not conformed to this world: but be ye transformed by the renewing of your mind, that ye may prove what is that good, and acceptable, and perfect will of God." Keep in mind that when scripture says "brethren," most scholars believe that is speaking to Christians. Therefore, in essence, this scripture is telling us we are to be a "living sacrifice" unto God. To understand what a sacrifice is supposed to be, we need to look at the sacrifices of old. Several scriptures (Exodus 12:5, Leviticus 1:3–10, Leviticus 4:23, etc.) tell us they are to be without spot or blemish. The Mosaic Law prohibited blemished persons from exercising the functions of the priests' office and prohibited the offering of blemished animals for sacrifice. The blemish was as imperfection, and this imperfection disqualified persons and things for sacred uses. It was intended to teach by this object lesson that no one whose heart was imperfect could enjoy the privileges of divine worship. Sacrifice is a basic aspect of man's approach to God, and the Christian approaches God under the sacrificial blood of Jesus Christ and reveals his participation in Christ by a sacrificial life. The sacrificial life is not to be judged by outward acts (works) but by inwardness, a total surrender to God. The sacrifice today is a death to sin and a new life in Christ.

We all know the sacrifice offered for our sins was Jesus, a male without spot or blemish. God required the children of old to make a spotless (perfect) sacrifice and tells us we are to be a "living sacrifice" and Christlike. Then He means that we are to live a spotless (sinless) life after we become a Christian.

I believe that some of the old hymns a lot of churches these days do not sing made this point in their inspired songs/words. Remember the song written by Charlotte Elliot in 1835, "Just as I Am." Let's look in particular at the words of the second verse: "Just as I am and waiting not to rid my soul of one dark blot, to thee whose blood can cleanse each spot, O Lamb of God, I come, I come." What is written is about cleansing from just *one* dark blot/sin. Some sin was not okay, not even *one*. Another classic was written by Robert Lowry in 1876 titled, "What Can Wash Away My Sin?" In verse 2, it states, "That makes me white as snow." That is as clean as clean can be. Many of those ole hymns were not just written; I believe they were inspired. Mistakes and temptations are going to happen as long as we are alive in this body. Sins, on the other hand, are avoidable by the keeping power of Christ. We can find this truth in Jude verses 24 and 25. It reads, "Now unto him that is able to keep you from falling (into sin) and present you faultless (without sin) before the presence of his glory with exceeding joy, To the only wise God our Savior, be glory and majesty, dominion and power, both now and ever. Amen." Jude understood the distinction between faults or mistakes and sins. In Christian perfection, mistakes and faults will disappear in the life to come, but we are to be saved from sins, not in sins now. I believe the decline of old hymns in our churches today may be, at least in part, attributed to their convicting, plain-speaking, inspired words that congregations don't want to hear. These old hymns make church attendees uncomfortable and exposes their hypocrisy.

Too many people are being taught that everyone sins, some every day, which is why when you listen to people pray, whether at church or at a meal at home, they have formed almost a habit tef saying, "Forgive me of my sins," or something along those lines. The Bible speaks of vain repetitions in prayers; look it up in Matthew 6:7. Most believe all you have to do is say, "I am sorry," and ask God to forgive you and you are good to go. Tomorrow they will do the same. As we have discussed earlier, there needs to be godly sorrow, a contrite spirit, and a broken heart. In other words, it is a very serious and sincere matter that is not to be taken lightly. Sin is serious. Romans 6:23 says, "The wages of sin is death." If we are taught (as most churches teach today) that it is impossible to live without sinning, some every day and over years of this type of teaching, we are convinced in our minds that it is impossible to live any other way. Why even try?

C. Grace

While we are here, I want to look at Romans 6:1 because we hear a lot today about the fact that we are living under *grace*. This is true, we are under grace. Some seem to believe and preach that because we are under grace, then if we do sin it is no big deal. Paul addresses this years ago in Romans 6:1, "What shall we say then? Shall we continue in sin, that grace may abound?" Then he answers his own question in the next verse, Romans 6:2, "God forbid." In my words, absolutely not, but then Paul tries to further explain with, "How shall we, that are dead to sin, live any longer therein?" In the verses that follow, he uses some commonsense questions and answers to make his point. Notice in the latter part of verse 6 he says, "We should not serve sin." Lastly on this point, in Romans 6 verse 7, we see "For he that is dead is freed from sin," which goes exactly along with what was said in John 8:32 and following. This is a verse that a lot of people like to quote. "And ye shall know the truth and the truth shall make you free." This verse is well-known and is heard a lot, but most stop there and don't continue to read the next few verses or, better yet, read the whole chapter and get the context. In verse 34, Paul tells us that we can be free from sin. It says,

"Verily, verily, I say unto you, whosoever committeth sin is the servant of sin." Understand that servants were not free. It seems quite obvious to me that he is saying if you know the truth, you can be free from sin. As we continue, let's look at Romans 6:20 while we are here. It says, "For when ye were [past tense] the servants of sin, ye were free from righteousness." Basically, you can't be both righteous and sinful. This ties directly back to what is said and we quoted earlier in this writing in Ezekiel 18:20–24. As I keep stating, it all ties in together like a jigsaw puzzle.

D. Placebo and Nocebo

Earlier I posed the question, why even try if it is impossible? Let me give you an example of how powerful the mind is.

Most people know what a placebo is. It is an inert substance or belief which produces real biological effects in humans. It is so widely accepted as fact that a placebo variable is included in most medical tests as a way of proving if, say, a drug works on its own merits or because people think it works. While placebos are generally associated with positive outcomes, like curing an illness, the nocebo effect produces negative effects. An instance of this happening would occur if someone broke out in a rash because they thought they touched poison ivy, even though it was merely an everyday ordinary plant.

In either case, the placebo and the nocebo effect are only as successful as the patient believing in them. This happens in most cases without the patient knowing the actual truth, only subconsciously knowing what the mind believes to be the truth.

One of the most talked about examples of the nocebo phenomenon was an incident published in the *New*

Scientist journal. According to the account, late one night, an Alabama man, referred to as Vance, went to a cemetery and met up with a witch doctor who told him that he was going to die soon. Believing the witch doctor's prediction, Vance soon fell ill and within a matter of weeks, was emaciated and close to death. Vance was taken to the hospital, but the doctors could not find anything wrong with him. Finally, Vance's wife told a doctor, Dr. Doherty, about the encounter with the witch doctor, which gave the creative physician an idea. The next day, Dr. Doherty told the couple he had tracked down the witch doctor and physically threatened him until the medicine man finally admitted he had put a lizard inside of Vance and the lizard was eating him from the inside. Of course, the doctor's story was completely fabricated, yet he made a big show of injecting the patient with a mysterious substance and snuck in a genuine green lizard that he pretended to extract from Vance. The next day, Vance awoke alert, hungry, and it didn't take long before he fully recovered.

There is another account I recently read about a man who submitted to a scientific hypnosis experiment. While under the influence of a light hypnotic trance, the subject was ordered to pick up a glass from the table. Although he was a strong, athletic type, the man could not budge the glass from its position. His most strenuous exertions could not lift the glass that was light enough for any child to remove.

Why could he not do it? Because the scientists, after placing him in the trance, had told him that it was impossible to pick up the glass. Because his mind was convinced that it could not be done, his body was unable to carry out the command to lift it. What a dramatic demonstration that no person can really obey commandments which he believes to be impossible to perform!

Just one final thought on how powerful our minds are, and one I think most people can relate to, is a dream. A dream occurs in our brain for most folks while they are sleeping. Most people, at one time or another, have had a dream where they woke up almost scared to death or with tears on their cheeks. During that time while experiencing it, it was like it was reality, but it was just a dream. That is just another example of how powerful our mind is. Don't ever underestimate its power!

Our thoughts, our beliefs, our faith—they are all closely related. Someone once said, "Our beliefs determine our actions." Jesus said in Matthew 17:20, "If you have faith like a grain of mustard seed, you will say to this mountain, 'Move from here to there, and it will move, and nothing will be impossible for you.'" Secular people have stated this differently, but it is similar. "Energy flows where attention goes" or "Focused thoughts focus energy, and energy moves energy." Our limits are clearly defined in the words of Jesus in Matthew 9:29 when He says, "According to your faith, be it unto you."

Because we are constantly told that we can't live without sinning, is this the reason so many Christians are living weak, defeated lives? There is no question that the popular, modern theology has been teaching millions that no one can really live without sinning. Many modern Christians are turning more and more to a soft, lenient stance on the subject of sin. They believe God's love is incompatible with strict rules and penalties for violation. Scripture tells us that at one point, it repented God that He had even created man and He was almost to the point of total destruction. Keep in mind the Bible says, in my words, "We were His best creation." Now let us pull into our destination on our journey to find the House of Truth.

RIGHTFUL DRIVEWAY

At this point, I hope, if nothing else, I have given you enough scriptural information to create an interest in you working out your own salvation through prayer and studying, paying close attention to what sayeth the word of God!

Everyone needs to read the account of the prodigal son found in Luke 15:11–24. This is a parable of a man who, according to a lot of scholars, was safe and sound in his father's house, but he wanted to control his own destiny. This is the point we each will reach at some point in our lives, maybe not physically but spiritually. He had some thoughts and ideas, and he dwelled upon them and devised a plan. He asked his father for his portion. Then we see in scripture where he "wasted his substance with riotous living." Scripture does not go into detail about what he actually did, but it just says, "when he had spent all, there arose a mighty famine in that land; and he began to be in want." This tells the whole story. He had lost it all, his money, his self-esteem, everything. Whose choice was this? It was his and his alone. This represents the sins that we choose, when we sin.

As we follow this parable, scripture tells us that he "came to himself." Some might say he "came to his senses," but no, the scripture wording carries more meaning. After he had come to himself, he was in a position to make some sound reasoning. He was in a pigpen, and that is as low as you can get, especially for a Jew. This is where sin will carry you. It may sound good and look good in the beginning, but the pigpen is where it will lead you!

It was at this point that he made the greatest decision of his life. He decided to go back to his father's house. The boy's confession of his mistake was necessary, just as repentance is necessary for you and me. The father represents God, He is ready to receive us back into the fold when we return, and He will clothe us with the robe of salvation. All that He requires is that we repent and return. Scripture tells us, "For this my son was dead, and is alive again; he was lost, and is found." This also is an example of the change that is supposed to occur—turn from your wicked ways!

This, friend, is a clear parable of what life is all about. Once you ask Jesus into your heart and are sincere and really mean it, you are safe in your Father's house. Then temptation comes along, and how we handle it will depend on whether it turns into sin or not. It is our choice. Once you make that decision, then we sin and become lost. Some people at this point will quote John 10:29, "My Father, which gave them to me, is greater than all; and no man is able to pluck them out of my Father's hand." Scripture is true and will never contradict itself; we need to understand what is being said here. No one else can pluck you out of the Father's hand—*only you can*! It will not be anybody else's fault, only yours. He will never force anything upon us. He is a gentleman, even more than any gentleman we have ever known. He gives us a free will, a will to make our own choices.

Remember this is a parable, and what is a parable? A parable is a simple story to provide a more profound lesson or teaching. In other words, parables are from the divine wisdom of Jesus Christ and are provided in order for us to learn everlasting truths in a common everyday simple form for better understanding.

I think another scripture that needs to be considered on this subject is the last two verses in the book of James 5:19–20. It reads, "Brethren, if any of you do err from the truth, and one convert him; Let him know, that he which converteth the sinner from the error of his way shall save a soul from death, and hide a multitude of sins." As has been said before, when the word *brethren* is used, it is talking to Christians. If you believe that we are all born into this world with inbred sin, and here they are called brethren, we have to assume they are Christians. Because of the err from the truth, you are now a sinner, but if someone converts you, then your soul is saved. Therefore, if you are not converted back, it indicates your soul would be lost.

Just some of these verses on their own should be enough to convince someone that if you believe the Bible to be the inerrant, inspired word of God, then it can't be that some of it is true and some not true; we have to believe all the scriptures. You undermine the whole Bible if you try and pick which verses you believe and which ones you don't believe. If you understand this to be true, then you better realize that you better not sin, and if you happen to on a rare occasion, we best ask God for forgiveness.

This is very important, and I do not want to be misunderstood. We have scripture where some have sinned/backslid or whatever term you want to use, but here is the heart of the matter: today it is taught by most pastors that it is an everyday occurrence. I do not find that in scripture! It should be taught that it should be the *rare* exception and not the daily rule. A lot of people use King David as an example, but understand, scripture only tells us of three sins David committed, not that he sinned every day. Too many people are being taught that everyone sins some every day, and that it is impossible to live without sinning some every day. Again, if we are convinced, in our minds, that Christian perfection is impossible, why try? I find not one verse that says that, but I find plenty that says, "Sin not." Sin is serious; sin is what separates us from God! It is impossible to serve two masters! You can't have it both ways! There are many verses in the scriptures that support this theology if we read it looking for the evidence and pray for God to give us the understanding.

Another short example is found in 1 Peter 5:8 where it says, "Be sober, be vigilant; because your adversary the devil, as a roaring lion, walketh about, seeking whom he may devour." This is where a little common sense comes into play or some may say, "good ole common horse sense." Two points I want to make here: First, if you are already in the devil's camp, so to speak, why would he be wasting his time seeking to devour you? He already has you, and you will be devoured. Second, if you are in the Lord's camp, then that would explain the devil's job is to try and entice you into sinning, and then you would forfeit your salvation and move into his camp. If this is not possible, why would scripture even mention that it could be done?

There are many other such scriptures, but I will just mention one in Revelation 3:5 which states, "He that over-cometh, the same shall be clothed in white raiment; and I will not blot out his name out of the book of life, but I will confess his name before my Father, and before his angels." What are we to overcome? *Sin!* It appears to indicate that, if we do not overcome, God will blot out our names out of the book of life. Now, if your name is in the book of life, you must be a Christian. Therefore, if your name is blotted out, you can forfeit your salvation.

Scriptures like these may indicate why Matthew 7:22–23 says, "Many will say to me in that day, 'Lord, Lord, have we not prophesied in thy name? And in thy name have cast out devils? And in thy name done many wonderful works? And then will I profess unto them, I never knew you: depart from me, ye that work iniquity." This balances out and makes perfect sense when we examine again the previous referenced scripture in Ezekiel 18:24.

I think a lot of the confusion and misunderstanding can be found in 1 Corinthians 2:14, "But the natural man receiveth not the things of the Spirit of God: for they are foolishness unto him: neither can he know them, because they are spiritually discerned." Natural unrepentant man cannot understand things that are only spiritually discerned through the prayer and studying of a repentant heart that ask God to give you understanding. Honestly, most people will say they do not have the time necessary to dedicate to this and that is what they pay the pastor to do, but that is where part of our modern-day sacrifice is today. We do not sacrifice animals, but we do have to sacrifice something—our time.

Today, it is not a lack of knowledge because, especially in America, we have easy access to a Bible and most have the availability of the internet, not to mention the numerous churches in most towns and communities. It is not a lack of time to study and learn for themselves. Most folks have an education, leisure time, and prosperity, so that is not the problem either. A friend of mine has often said, "If you really think about it, we have it better today than Solomon in all his glory. We have automatic cold air and warm heat and easy access to food and medicine. We are richly blessed as a people/nation." Men in times of prosperity have a tendency to forget God, relax, and become complacent. They begin to, almost unconsciously, put their trust and faith in their wealth, insurance, and self, believing these things that they have worked hard for will afford them peace and happiness. The results are almost always the same. After a time, a flood of evil comes because man, apart from God, disintegrates into a monster of self-destruction. This not only goes for a man but for a church or a nation as a whole.

Are you going to choose what the Bible says or what Bro. So and So says? It is your choice and yours alone. Choose salvation and live a perfect Christian life without sinning every day. See, today not many believe this, but scripture says in Luke 13:23–24, someone asked Jesus the question, "Are there few that be saved?" His answer is, "Strive to enter in at the strait gate: for many, I say unto you, will seek to enter in, and shall not be able." This I believe is why scripture tells us at judgment He will say, "Depart from me, I never knew you." Once we forfeit our salvation, all goodness is forgotten! If you have any doubt, you need to make sure you know where you are going to spend eternity.

I have endeavored to base everything I have written here on the Bible. The Bible, generally speaking, has always been and will always be a rather disagreeable book to men in many respects and will irritate their minds and hearts because it is fashioned according to their understanding, but it is an indictment of it. There are churches in every age that is a product of this attempt to make religion pleasing to man and his reason, to conform it to his norms and standards, but it is man who must be conformed to God and his word. In most churches today, the net results of all reasonable religion is that it becomes a house of fraud. It has been conformed to the wickedness of a fallen creature and is accordingly fallen and fraudulent. A lot of churches and faiths based on nothing or fraud flourish and abound because they cater and appeal to the sinful nature of man. Also, for all their seeming prosperity, they are weak because power resides in only the true church of God, which alone has "the victory that overcometh the world," as stated in 1 John 5:4. What we have today is what Timothy described in 2 Timothy 3:5, "Having a form of godliness, but denying the power thereof: from such turn away."

I did not write this and spend this time to create stress, division, or indecision. I wrote this in the hopes of giving scriptural based evidence of why a lot of people are being led astray, and I just ask that you find the answers to your questions from scripture and not let your eternity depend on someone else's interpretation. You and you alone will have to answer at judgment. God is a loving God and He does not want anyone to spend eternity in torment in hell. Maybe this is why you read this book. I hope you have enjoyed your visit, and I wish you would sincerely stay at the House of Truth. I want to thank you for your time, and may God lead, guide, and direct your path. In Jesus's name, amen.

ABOUT THE AUTHOR

Ted Everett has sold everything from pine cones to pine boxes. Being one of six children growing up in south Mississippi as a preacher's kid and having over twenty-five years in the cemetery/funeral business, he has seen and heard a lot. This background inspired his inquisitive mind to do some investigating on his own.

Since his three children have all grown and gone, he likes learning new things if he isn't gardening or golfing. He lives in north Alabama with his lovely wife, looking forward to enjoying those "golden years."

www.ingramcontent.com/pod-product-compliance
Lightning Source LLC
Chambersburg PA
CBHW021149130726
47988CB00004B/1531